Cusp

Cusp

Jennifer Grotz

A MARINER ORIGINAL
Houghton Mifflin Company
Boston • New York
2003

I thank my entire family, and I am deeply grateful to the individuals and institutions that supported and encouraged me during the writing of this book. Chin "Roland" Chong, Michael Collier, David Daniels, Tenaya Darlington, Ted Genoways, Landon Godfrey, Chris Green, Sarah Griffin, Gary Hawkins, Kristin Henderson, Edward Hirsch, A. Van Jordan, Yusef Komunyakaa, Judith Montgomery, Glen Moore, Carl Phillips, Patrick Phillips, Michael Robins, Bruce Smith, Shirley Stephenson, Ellen Bryant Voigt, David Wojahn, C. Dale Young, and Adam Zagajewski—*thank you*. Mountain Writers Series, Literary Arts, Inc., the Oregon Arts Commission, Inprint, Inc., and most importantly, the Bread Loaf Writers' Conference— *thank you*.

This book is for Joshua Keen, loving keeper of innumerable keys.

Library of Congress Cataloging-in-Publication Data

Grotz, Jennifer.

Cusp / Jennifer Grotz.

p. cm.

"A Mariner original."

ISBN 0-618-30246-8

I. Title.

PS3607.R675C87 2003

811'.6—dc21 2003042023

Printed in the United States of America

Book design by Robert Overholtzer

WIZ 10 9 8 7 6 5 4 3 2 1

I would like to thank the editors of the following journals for publishing the following poems (sometimes in slightly different versions): *Black Warrior Review:* "The Train, 2" (published as "The Train"). *Brilliant Corners:* "Jazz in Paris." *Cimarron Review:* "Virginity," "Fish." *Clackamas Literary Review:* "Mind of Winter." *Crab Orchard Review:* "Summary," "Last of the Imperials." *Hayden's Ferry Review:* "Ceramics." *Hubbub:* "Dear John Bunyan." *The Kenyon Review:* "Arrival in Rome." *Meridian:* "Lust." *New England Review:* "Last Living Castrato," "Between Dog and Wolf," "The Floating World," "The Waves," "Le Bel Été," "Self-Portrait as a Drowned Man." *Phoebe:* "Self-Portrait as Annunciation." *Pleiades:* "The Train." *Ploughshares:* "Waiting to Wake Up Française." *Portland Review:* "Inevitable." *Puerto del Sol:* "Not This Raw Fluttering." *Sycamore Review:* "First Glasses." *TriQuarterly:* "Map to Light You Can Call Blue," "Kiss of Judas." "Last Living Castrato" appeared in *The Best American Poetry 2000,* guest edited by Rita Dove. "Map to Light You Can Call Blue," "Unknown," "Dear John Bunyan," "Cusp," "Inevitable," and "Glimpse" appeared in *Not Body,* a limited edition letterpress chapbook produced by Urban Editions, December 2001.

Souvent dans le silence d'un ravin
J'entends (ou je désire entendre, je ne sais)
Un corps tomber parmi des branches. Longue et lente
Est cette chute aveugle; que nul cri
Ne vient jamais interrompre ou finir.

Je pense alors aux processions de la lumière
Dans le pays sans naître ni mourir.

Often in the silence of a ravine
I hear (or I long to hear, I don't know which)
A body falling through the branches. Long and slow
Is this blind fall; no cry
Ever comes to interrupt or end it.

I think then of light's procession
In the country without birth or dying.

—Yves Bonnefoy, "Le Bel Été"

CONTENTS

Foreword by Yusef Komunyakaa   ix

I
Between Two Road Signs in Northern Territory   3
The Floating World   4
The Last Living Castrato   6
Map to Light You Can Call Blue   7
Fish   8
Virginity   10
Glimpse   11
Ceramics   12
First Glasses   14
Alizarin Crimson   16
The Waves   17

II
Try   21
Le Bel Été   22
The Ladder   23
Not This Raw Fluttering   24
Lust   25
Last of the Imperials   27
Tarantismus   28
Unknown   30
Joshua Bell to His Violin   31
Kiss of Judas   32

III
Self-Portrait as a Drowned Man   35
Waiting to Wake Up *Française*   37
Dear John Bunyan,   39
Jazz in Paris   41
Boulevard Slick with Rain   43
Arrival in Rome   45

IV
The Train   51
Summary   52
Cusp   53
Self-Portrait as *Annunciation*   54
The Wolf   56
The Train, 2   57
Mind of Winter   58
Inevitable   59
Elegy   60
Between Dog and Wolf   62

JENNIFER GROTZ's first full-length collection, *Cusp*, opens on the edge of an illusionary terrain, with "Between Two Road Signs in Northern Territory," a time and place where the speaker says, "I am thinking of the exit into daylight, // it fools me every time, sunlight a harsher seduction" and "nighttime / robs the day, speeding nighttime." In this place, opposites seem to merge and render clarity to vision and possibility.

Where many first books seem like a jumble of titles and images, off kilter to the heart's alignment, *Cusp* is almost seamless in tone and structure. And yet, numerous surprises are embedded in these pages. The first poem expertly prepares us for the second, "The Floating World," for phrases such as

> Finding *now* is the cult of the floating world, but now we are
> so poisoned
>
> and drowsy from perfume and fear. Even my body behaves like
> a question
> increasingly impatient at no answer. I am the firefly catcher in
> the woodblock

These poems, one after another, magnify the landscapes where the mute and static are propelled into artful motion — the inanimate exists on the cusp of active knowledge, in a new world, at the edge of desire's fulfillment and completion. There's a heartfelt quest at the center of each poem, an attempt to diminish disbelief, to make time concrete, as is brilliantly underscored in "Unknown":

> Like a spider suspended
> from a beam, the moment
> swayed. The silk
> of the web was invisible.
> Belief seemed an unlikely thing.

And the spider herself was monstrous,
a spotted bulb with transparent legs
sharp as hooks. She fidgeted in midair,

plucked the strings of the web
to re-create a keyhole,
to make herself
the key into the next passage.

One of Grotz's many gifts is this: she knows how to wed emotion
to mystery without abstracting the imagery and language. The mys-
tery vibrates like a plucked string in the darkness.

Perhaps the speakers in this collection begin at the cusp, but each
undergoes a transformation. Thus, we as attentive readers are also
changed. Many of these poems are about the making of art, the see-
ing into phenomenon, and the depiction of our desires as women and
men, as artists. Take, for example, the introductory two stanzas of
"Joshua Bell to His Violin":

This is what I hear when you begin to dip
and quiver: I have one hundred lit candles
to blow out. Then my throat grows sore,
tightens while oxygen passes through it,

and the candles throb like manic petals
jealous of the music my arm releases from you.

On the cusp of multiple borders, the speakers throughout this
wonderful collection find the strength and integrity to cross borders
in the flesh and mind—one half-hidden path leads to another, and
before long, without any deception, a certain transcendence is earned
through Grotz's vibrant language.

Though this poet's canvas is expansive, moving the reader through
varied landscapes, from "Between Two Road Signs in Northern Terri-

tory" to "Jazz in Paris," West Texas is always pulsating underneath the wrought language. Sometimes the speakers of these illuminated tableaus are transported through dreams, and other times the narrators are wheeled through time and space by trains, cars, horses, and the gritty wit of observation and experience of the road. And yes, also by leaps of faith in mystery, where a speaker gazes in multiple directions simultaneously. Such is the case highlighted in the first couplets of the last poem in *Cusp*, "Between Dog and Wolf":

> I can't help but look back: piles of rusted stakes
> half buried in the ground which gives after the melt.
>
> The train cars are disconnected, paralyzed
> on their tracks, empty but for cold. The train
>
> is dangerous and sleepy. I listen for its two
> appearances which fill my upstairs room:
>
> the tired horns of 5 P.M., hazy with downtown traffic
> and the heartbreaking roar of its 1 A.M. passage.

Out of the sacred territory of poetry, that country within a body politic that often seems murky and indefinable, every now and then emerges a voice true to its tradition, conveying a music and imagery that are unique. In Jennifer Grotz's *Cusp*, paths cross and cultures collide softly, and women and men tantalize each other until connections occur, leaving behind joy and hurt, but never abandonment. There's nothing giddy or immature in these glancing blows; sincerity resides in the nervous system of each poem—where speakers exist on the cusp of possible happiness. The regrets are few in this immense landscape, as if driven by a frontier spirit: the next river to cross, the next obstacle to endure, and the next dream to weave into perspective. One landscape might remind a speaker of another secret experience, so empathic travel is created. And the farther each speaker is propelled out among the stars, the more earthbound he or she becomes. Though the characters who appear in this spellbinding collection don't remind us of some high-plains drifter, West Texas is still close to the bone of Grotz's vision. And it is more than the strange, winding territory of the heart.

YUSEF KOMUNYAKAA

I

Between Two Road Signs in Northern Territory

Allumez vos phares the road sign warns
as I enter the tunnel, where nighttime

robs the day, speeding nighttime.
A kilometer later a sign will remind me

Vos phares? but for this instant, litter scrapes and flutters
across the ground and I am thinking of the exit into daylight,

it fools me every time, sunlight a harsher seduction
than the gleaming eyes of cars rippling behind.

Overhead lights stream geometric shadows
that could be pines. In the center of the tunnel

where entrance disappears, I have no choice.
The story is the same backward and forward

so the story is not the point. And the tunnel whispers
go down, it whirs and hums. It is the projector's hiss,

the seat that reclines. I drive deep into the *now*
of the tunnel: after the light behind recedes

my dashboard glows, intricate, boxed in glass.
I dare not interrupt, I spend my fire . . .

The Floating World

The huge quick bursts of light grow like time lapse photography
and dissolve into darkness and embers trailing into black water.

I will find you here, sudden as fireworks blooming
above the river, the light rail blurring through the empty street,

past the grand hotels along the waterfront, where you stand
momentarily breathless amid brass and thick carpet, I know this,

while bellboys rake the vast ashtrays, stamping the hotel insignia
   on white sand.
Amid the corrosive rain of fireworks, I wonder who would ever
   leave you.

Who could bear to bloom and fade from you? Earlier in sunlight
we found a demolished building between two skyscrapers.

A boom truck, yellow and toy-like, balanced on the collapsed floors,
everything coated with the fine pink dust of crumbled brick. I know
   an anchor

must be here, amid the world floating with all its lights and teases,
the carnival spread out like a strip mall along the river, the highways

forming concrete orbits, tracing the many paths we've taken to
   arrive.
The parking lot off Burnside fills with the Japanese woodblock of
   the King of Hell

surrounded by his Attendants. The anxiousness of people waiting
   for the bus.
Finding *now* is the cult of the floating world, but now we are so
   poisoned

and drowsy from perfume and fear. Even my body behaves like a
    question
increasingly impatient at no answer. I am the firefly catcher in the
    woodblock

where my mistress in her starry robe holds a fan and paper lantern
with two crooked pinkies as I lunge for the veined night sky

with hand raised to grasp—moonlight's clichéd now—
at the haloed black insects, five of them lazily floating.

The Last Living Castrato

Difficult to believe, a knife ensures the voice,
soprano notes proceed intact while chest hair and beard
accompany the new lower octaves, the voice expanding

beyond sex, limited only by lung. And now whole
operas composed for castrati are abstract and
unperformable, now whole species of off-humans who

were sacrificed for air, for air sinking and rising
in their throats, are extinct, now facsimiles
reproduce for our ears what is digital mastery,

bleeding soprano and countertenor. Except for
the brief miracle of Edison's recording:
the last living castrato's voice brimming through

static and hiss. Technology at its beginning and
old-school opera at its decline, that cusp
between where a voice spanning five octaves sang

to give us proof of the voice, and of how
we doctored it to make it more whole, to widen
emotion's aperture. He held it

in his mouth. Audiences would beg for
the aria to be sung over and over,
interrupting the story, which was only

an excuse for the voice. The voice is *how*,
rising, rising, so as to dive,
and he held it in his mouth releasing

our cruel sacrifice, our gratitude
to hear it fall, driven to where
the voice takes us: silence, applause.

Map to Light You Can Call Blue

Where crows gather in military V's
    to stitch the unhealable wound of sky.
They spiral into Lake Ransom Canyon before dusk,
    their cries echoing on caliche, *abandon.*
Start here, where fields of cotton mop the caprock dust
    that released at your birth.

The oily road leads you to wildflower
    graves, then back to this dust
suspended in the sunset at your feet.
    Will this much dust be miraculous, splintered
earth in air? When it settles, wipe it off
    the car hood as if this weren't Texan desert
but what will seem impossible, what will
    never stop astonishing.

Spangled. Purple. Ruined.
    I want the words to get me back to you.
The crows ruin my entrance. They sing their spangled
    ohhhs until the purple night makes
foamy ash of you. Because I cannot
    stop you, I let the sunset envelop you.

But now the desert and the canyon are lunar surfaces, and
    you are unforgivable.
When will you turn suspicious? New one, is it enough
    to love the alien land and not to know later
you will love a man this way, grasp
    his arm as terribly as this terrain
resists gathering you up?

Fish

Leaves in Lubbock curl
    into dark hands, fall
into yellow grass, but the desert reasserts itself
    every season. Because October is not
the time of dying, because everything is tentative
    planted in dust, flat land packs itself
tighter. Where the most alien thing to imagine
    is water roaring underground
through the pumps of the Ogalalla Aquifer,
    a sky turns powdery and bright.

Under this light we huddled at the pond
    by the concrete underpass
with muddy string and carrots to lure crawfish.
    Unpredictable, unaware of season,
the minnows darted, changed direction
    like the roaches swimming across sugar packets
in the hatchback parked next door
    stuffed completely except for the driver's seat
with trash. A lake of old cereal boxes
    and junk mail, crusty towels and fast-food cups
pressed against the windows.

I have defined my landscape by its shapes, the family
    car's four doors ajar in the driveway
like a cruel piece of farm machinery,
    or my friend who listens to Mahler
with long pieces of stiff paper
    he folds up or down
to make a skyline for each symphony.
    But what of a fish in water, more abstract
than music, yes, soundless until caught,
    then frantic and vowel-like?

What of its ceaseless stare—but I must stop
  because the fish belongs where it is supple and limbless.
Biologists argue over what makes a school: two or three
  or as many as form a three-dimensional shape.
In fall, the dying fits in: I picture the pond
  dribbling into the packed mud and grassy edge.
The hatchback holds this shape, and shape is this tentative—
  it has gaps and tiny spaces, never filled—
while the fish is smothered in water, its skeleton
  flimsy as plastic price tags, and that is
terrifying, or am I looking all wrong?

Virginity

Tornadoes keep West Texas flat. Tornadoes kept me after school
    crouched with my peers on the same cement floor
of the hallway Buddy Holly once (legend has it) rode his
    motorcycle through. One-story buildings, low-swinging
stoplights. Afternoons when a clear
    sky fattens with bruised clouds. Nights
a Thomas Hardy novel in all its naive countryside
    could absolve me in a smoky all-night coffee shop.
I lived a velvety fear, a pull in my chest like thirst.

    Sometimes I'd drive the highway thirty miles from town,
mesmerized by the cotton-colored streetlamps,
    strips of light climbing the hood, the windshield
—over and beyond the car—looping road
    and my concentration at getting farther away, my faith
in the highway's curving. That's the way
    it worked, then. Counting the men who would agree
to meet me past midnight behind the church.
    Did I actually look into their faces?

I had to tell myself I'd never come back
    to the neon-lit gas stations,
to a cowboy staring hard at a drop of diesel splashed
    on my sandal, to that desert where things shriveled,
disintegrated into bits you could give away.
    The swarms of eighteen-wheelers rumbled by me,
their countless lights winking in complicity.
    They passed ahead.
I never wondered at their cargo.

Glimpse

Chest-deep in water at Corpus Christi,
I feel a jellyfish brush past my thighs
like a silk scarf floating through the waves.

When I plunge my head underwater and
feel the tightness in my chest begin,
I open my eyes: an indistinct blue
and a constant pressure to rise

which I inevitably do.
Fish jerk and shiver away until only the faceless remain,
bits of seaweed clumped like Magdalen's long wet hair.

Again, I hold my breath and push down to the bottom,
the sand's blurry diamonds, soft dunes, rocks composed
like gardens. I grab a handful
to inspect above. Silk drains into a gritty clay.

Inside shells, milky oysters secrete their pearls.
Blood remains under the surface like ink
before language, until the skin breaks

and blood beads up like a question.
Until the sting raises welts. What stilled me,
kept me from wrapping the scarf underwater around
my neck? To glimpse anything more.

Ceramics

Somewhere Grandmother is talking a yardman's ear off,
    persuading him to build a crucifix
        in the backyard. She's thinking

he'll bless the tomato plants, holy scarecrow.
    It's not that Grandmother grew up in Oklahoma,
        it's just that she was more comfortable lodged between

two men in the front seat of a pickup truck,
    men she'd call gentlemen, men nice enough
        to pull to the side of the road when she asked

so she could go pee in the brush and pull
    her underwear quickly back up. *Bloomers.*
        She called anything white for the legs bloomers.

She was a terrible cook, always confusing ingredients,
    salt instead of sugar. I think of food back then as dusty
        greenware in the garage, slip congealing

in milk jugs, fat rubber bands sticking to our heels
    as we'd wander shelves of plaster molds
        for something to paint and fire in the kiln,

something to glaze and burn. That silver hexagon
    on stilts Mother put on top of the dryer
        with porcelain cones to plug the holes —

and when she'd check to see if our greenware
    was bisque, the 600-degree glow on her face and hands,
        a radiation of love. I'd bore

holes into the hollow cups and figurines, scrape
    away the soft seams and sponge them smooth, chisel
        my name or my love on the unpainted base, watch

the moisture leave it gray. While the tomatoes fattened
　　in the triangular patch of a corner lot, while the dogs
　　　　sank their teeth into them, still green,

ate them whole, even buried them, I always felt in trouble.
　　Grandmother preached a lot, fingered the cross around her neck.
　　　　She was what my parents called a holy roller. She wouldn't let me

slurp with a spoon. I begged to go to the "turned-on"
　　churches with her, envisioning something to do with divine
　　　　rollerskating, but instead I ended up huddled under the front pew,

hiding from the heavy mismatched footsteps
　　of parishioners speaking in tongues, eyes rolling back,
　　　　hands swaying, as if they'd tasted something awful. Their necks

went stiff, brittle enough, I thought, to snap.

First Glasses

He told me what I could see twenty feet away
others could see clearly from eighty.
Driving home from downtown we took
the back road studded with crabapples
my brother and I threw from the narrow height
of the school bus windows, my left hand
clutching the spelling bee word list:
McGee's Egg Stop, the cemetery, then
the quilted fields. There was never enough
to read in the afternoons—the *TV Guide*,
free magazines picked up in Tom Thumb
with listings for houses. Mother always
itched to move, and I loved boxing up
toys and records, fighting with my brother
for the biggest bedroom almost once a year.
I read phone books, dictionaries, and rummaged
the kitchen junk drawer where Mother kept
her greeting cards, their rhymes penned by no one,
almost personal in their printed cursive.
Even then I knew what was handwritten meant
more than the Hallmark script, although
Mother read each line regardless,
sometimes two or three times, needing
sentiment enough to read the words
as though they were truly the right ones,
the necessary, meant ones, as if
her heart could focus to fit the card.
Bedtime reading was the Bible
I'd open after dinner until my father found me
hours later, asleep. He'd pick the book up,
place it in my bed, say a Bible on the floor
was sacrilege. That year the local paper
pictured me in my new glasses,
with a headline that read, "Spell 'Scoundrel.'"

I lost the spelling bee by mistaking "scoundrel"
for "scandal," and spelled, I read that night,
"a publicized incident that brings about disgrace
or offends the moral sensibilities of society."
I didn't know, but I felt disgrace, a girl's
uncombed awkwardness, clumsy nightly navigations
down the hallway for water. Kids at school
called me Scoundrel for the few months we remained,
and none of us knew what it meant
until I looked it up to find I was a villain,
a rogue, an unreliable person. The Old Testament
defined it "sinner," and I remember trembling
as Mother and I left the optometrist's office.
New-eyed, I saw each leaf, suddenly dangerous as a razor,
capable as any of us of drawing blood.

Alizarin Crimson

The color of blood, as I remember,
the smell of medicine I inhaled
as Mother twisted off the cap

and squeezed a dollop on the palette.
She painted a field in West Texas
with a barn a farmer had stained red

with buttermilk and iron oxide.
In back of her storefront on 34th Street,
housewives came for evening classes,

set up easels in a circle,
ate spice cake with red-hots
bleeding into stiffened icing.

The paint was bright enough to eat,
smeared brilliantly on my thumb.
It lined the whorls of my fingers.

Other colors I loved: cobalt
and ultramarine blue, but none
sounded like a dress with reptilian layers.

Brushes stroked petals, welts, soft bruises.
No matter how dark the night was, no matter
how shiny the beetle, close looking showed

the reds and blues. Black never
went onto a canvas but alizarin crimson
hid in tulips, rooftops, and sky.

The Waves

The lips snarling, curling in disgust
The scrolling, the unwinding of a page, a page that resists falling flat
The sensation of falling, of falling through falling until it's floating,
     dissipation, erosion
The way from a car one watches the hills come forward, a slow swell
     on the ribbon of road that stretches forever
Or how buildings collapse, as if to their knees, tilting slightly to the
     side, swallowed in smoke

Half mirror, half magic carpet, undulating above the sand
The tug of war when one side of the rope lets go or the way
A woman smoothes the dress over her hips, presses down the
     wrinkles or shakes loose the folds gathered while she sat
Hundreds of white swans, agitated swans
So futile, inevitable, umbrageous, annihilating

Like the braggart, the hyperbolist, the endless deferrals—
Ever more, a little more,
The person who endlessly repeats himself, repeats not to be heard,
     just to stir the silence that must be interrupted . . .
A fizz, an effervescence, a mercurial carbonation

Quick like fire it travels, climbs up the shore to lick
     the large black log sinking into the sand
The way like fire it washes over, cleans and purifies to ash, to
     foaming undertow, dark roiling that never surfaces
Like the birds swooping and circling, the crow's silvery extension of
     wings, and the springing up of the tree's branches

And then like this: that a feeling arises because now and then the
     waves come up to unbutton the stones from the sand
Because the pouring becomes so voluminous and fierce
     it's a curtain pulling the windows and the house down

That we too want to be pulled down, licked over, left to dry
    atop glitter and seaweed

And this above all: we are not mountains, nor like them

And this: that we die terribly, pushing our bodies against winds

And then the sand trembles under our footsteps

II

Try

"Try to praise the mutilated world." — Adam Zagajewski

To love the world is what you try to do,
describe the trash, the bombs, the fisted greed—
when it does not love back, does not love you.

There are still breezes, kisses, and a few
more pleasures between gratitude and need.
To love the world is what you try to do

after seeing the slow old man pursue
in the parking lot a cart that gathers speed.
When it does not love back, does not love you,

the world seems like a hammer and a screw.
Aside from watch and act, can one succeed
to love the world? What they say's untrue,

that what you do won't matter. View
the world as a book that needs to be reread
when it does not love back, does not love you.

Or, watch it like a candle troubled into blue
under a fan, a candle filigreed
to love the world. It's what you try to do
when it does not love back, does not love you.

Le Bel Été

after Yves Bonnefoy

That summer, you practiced saying goodbye to God
By leaning into shadows and breezes, like the trees
That quivered in hushed breaths along the boulevard

That led to the river of bridges.
Light pressed against doors and soaked through windows.
Leaves on the plum tree shook cherry-stained shadows.

The cat stuttered a cry at the bird's hops and head turns.
Death would not stop invading our hearts.
It was summer, strange, unending, wakeful.

You loved the sadness that lived above the city, the clouds
That dulled the river to verdigrised metal.
Each bridge lifted out of a backbend

To let the hundred-eyed boats pass through.
Sometimes, when I stare into the river,
I see a woman (or is it only a dress, I don't know)

Rising to the surface. Its floating ripples into a bas-relief
of a statue's drapery fanning endlessly in the water.
Time inches across the heavy earth. We change so quietly.

The Ladder

"I want! I want!" cries the figure climbing up the skinny ladder,
such a long climb to be filled with wanting, such a long

shadow cast onto the surface of the ground
while the ladder sips like a straw from the moon

it leads to, here as tiny as a rind of fingernail, suspended
in the night William Blake scratched and darkened

save for seven fuzzy stars. It looks like punishment:
you hook your leg on the third rung and look up,

such a long climb for what you lack. It *must* be said twice
to show how saying does not in fact release it.

Perhaps, after climbing, you will reach the reclining crescent
and sleep upon it like a hammock before you realize that home

is the barren moon below: beautiful, light-reflecting,
but missing you. And if wanting is a ladder between

two moons, then the stars will hang neglected.
Surely Blake made the print no larger than a playing card

so that the ladder could lean without tearing
a paper sky gently pierced by stars.

Not This Raw Fluttering

Oversunned daffodils on the dashboard,
muddied yellow skirts quivering
the scent of a horse let out of stables
to graze a field. I could forget flowers,
the dandelions he fastened into bracelets.
Trying to see them beautiful, I could almost forget
their wilting. I press them to my eyelids,
dusted with pollen, hopelessly gravel-blind.
What startles is the way I no longer flinch
when he speaks of the terrible finish, panicked
so long now I'm filled with twisted
spokes. And still this rise in the stomach
at his now-sudden movements, like the Guatemalan
children my friend describes who throw
firecrackers all afternoon just to keep warlike
sounds in their heads, the way pain comforts
when it's all we know, remembering.
All these remnants left inside from when
the windshield caved in, glittering on my lap.
I'm not finished talking about fire,
the glass in my fingers, damning
the way it's embedded in the steering
wheel, how it makes me afraid to switch
directions. I've hardly begun cataloguing
the leftover kisses on the dashboard:
west kiss, kiss of his elbow bent, climbable kiss,
kiss half kissed, lonely kiss, holy kiss, kissless
kiss, kiss of the improbable, diamond kiss,
wandering kiss, kiss for the out-of-mind.

Lust

I loved to watch him buck
and bounce on the bareback horses,
his hand roped to the mouth

until he dared release.
I was seventeen. Every weekend
I went to the Fort Worth rodeo

to watch his cowboy hat fill with dust
while I shelled bags of peanuts,
washed down with syrupy Dr Pepper.

I'm not like Tina, who only dates
musicians. She says she sees
a calloused hand slide down

an upright bass and thinks: he can
do that to me. Sometimes the sex
would hurt — my hips would bruise,

red welts rose on my shoulders and back.
Too much about the rodeo I'll never
understand, save that I'm spellbound

by broncos and calves, the herding
and roping. He left me for a rodeo clown,
famous for her bucket tricks. I moved

to Plano, became a secretary, quit
eating TV dinners. I was almost twenty
when his back snapped, trampled by a horse.

When his mother called she said,
"I always thought you two would marry."
I threw away my blond wig. He hadn't

told her about the clown. I was
modeling small-time on weekends,
and I wore a dress from the Easter layout

at Neiman's to the funeral. All the old
guys were there, hanging their tanned heads
like ripe apples. They took turns

offering me their flasks. That's where I stop
when I tell this to impress my girlfriends.
It's how the story should end, as that's all it is now,

loose truth, the thud of his body on the pavement
outside the bowling alley, where we
went to split a pitcher, practice

the pleasing crash of ball to pins,
each reset a sterile hope. And somehow they want
Pete to be a hero, not a victim of a hit-and-run.

A broncobuster charges desire. And the rodeo,
my best metaphor for lust, betrays the way
what's natural leaps into performance.

Last of the Imperials

The announcer for each heat
praises the lime-green car
screeching its way into the pit—
this baby is one of the last
of the Imperials, a Chrysler
so full of metal it could be
used today to make three sedans.
Underneath the spray paint
and yellow exhaust, there's architecture
to this gas guzzler, making the El Camino
in the corner painted *Cracker Jack 49*
look like a true underdog.

At the derby everything takes place
in slow motion and mud. Bumpers drag and gleam
until rear-ended into accordions,
abandoned like gum wrappers.
Past curled hoods and concave fenders,
past all four tires wilting flat or slithering off entirely,
twisted like fat rubber bands,
these jalopies bulldoze toward the end.
Now an engine goes ablaze
and all the cars stop while yellow-suited firemen
run in with extinguishers.

Atop their smoking hoods, the drivers
spread their arms above the arena littered with debris
like the finale of an aria. We cheer
like connoisseurs of the Baroque,
Portuguese for misshapen pearl.
Pearl we elegize and crunch into dust.

Tarantismus

"Don't panic," he blurts as we curl together
   near sleep in his twin bed. Selena is out,
      his rose-haired tarantula,

and he's already on his knees inspecting the carpet.
   Weeks ago he superglued some twigs and rocks
      to make her home in a glass tank.

I think he wants me to hold her sometimes
   but I'm afraid. Each of her legs has a little claw
      to suction onto a surface

and when I imagine that tug, the crawl on the skin,
   the near-tickle creates an urge to dance,
      to shake out the arms, kick the legs.

He lets her out in the evenings to explore
   his arms and shoulders, then retreat to dark corners.
      Medieval Italians believed tarantula bites caused madness

and uncontrollable dancing. He knows
   she'll never show loyalty or even recognition,
      that she's ancient careful legwork

that needs heat to survive. This is the first thing
   I learn about him: he knows how to love what can't
      love back. Eventually she will molt

and we'll watch her begin by webbing a cocoon
   and leave her body behind, emerge pinker and larger
      from a perfect replica of herself.

He'll keep it in a jelly jar and we'll admire it,
  bristly haired, slinking fingers. But now he's naked,
    on his hands and knees and gingerly

uncovering our abandoned clothes. I'm on my knees too,
  lifting rumpled blankets where arm and leg carry joy or fear
    a step removed from the dance.

Unknown

Like a spider suspended
from a beam, the moment
swayed. The silk
of the web was invisible.
Belief seemed an unlikely thing.

And the spider herself was monstrous,
a spotted bulb with transparent legs
sharp as hooks. She fidgeted in midair,

plucked the strings of the web
to re-create a keyhole,
to make herself
the key into the next passage.

Nothing seemed apparent.
The breeze moved through the keyhole.
I wanted to flatten
against a wall like a moth.
Two lips holding back a cry.

Joshua Bell to His Violin

This is what I hear when you begin to dip
and quiver: I have one hundred lit candles
to blow out. Then my throat grows sore,
tightens while oxygen passes through it,

and the candles throb like manic petals
jealous of the music my arm releases from you.

I am so young my bones have made a place
for you, my wrist bends, my neck crooks to hold
your shallow body like a teenager balances a phone.
Stradivarius, sometimes I enact a sonorous trembling,

bangs convulsing around my face, the audience
coughing, you with your misery and me to get it out.

I do not know where it comes from,
that wind. You were shaped to help
its arrival, an emblem of grief, not the grief itself.
The sound leaves before we can change it.

This time a woman has caught the sound and holds it
in her throat. I confess it is only a way to understand

the music's loss, but no one is ever merely
vessel, violin, your smooth wood stained
the color of dried blood and my chin locking you
against my neck. I cradle you.

Toppling beauty: the candles require air and you
give them wind until they flicker and smoke.

Kiss of Judas

It's not greed I feel in me, the silver in my pocket
slapping my thigh like knives (*I know I am about to die*)
but the knowledge my kiss will betray you, betray me (*I welcome*
this kiss, I want it on my lips, I want to hear its click)
when I cup your chin in my hand, when I stare in your eyes
(*I am frightened by my Father, by my Judas, who comes*
sheepishly toward me through the crowd of soldiers)
I am unsure it could be more full than this moment,
I am so fearful of heaven, the grand cacophony of spears
jabbing skyward around us, torches blazing light in your face,
a redundancy (*I love his dark skin and how his robe swings*
heavy, how he has caught me) They were dirty men to deal with,
they hate you, they are jealous (*why am I only love?*)
Find me your truest of all, I could be years
but not eternity (*please come kiss me*) I am drawn toward
a destruction (*I want to be generous*), and if I cry
I know you forgave me before they counted coins
into my palm (*give myself to this inevitable,*
to someone oblivious in his unasking), before Peter losing
his temper (*I will replace the ear*) Loss is
what is irreplaceable (*rise to this moment and say,*
I let you go and be and may you be pleased) So obvious in words
(*not control of him, not word of him, not hope of him, but*
permission) I will kiss the savior (*every muscle relaxed now*)
but I am not the one who matters (*I am to be erased,*
so that I might exist somewhere else, present but)
you will push me (*like music, no traces of it afterward*)
gently away, seal us apart (*I chose him knowing his love*
would be painful, would make my heart heavy and anxious
for this to pass) and I am not sure how much
longer I will linger (*Both of us shall be wretched*)

III

Self-Portrait as a Drowned Man

So hard to keep the body still, early photography studios
were torture chambers, filled with devices to hold the body

long enough for the film to be exposed, and so when
Hippolyte Bayard took off his shirt, aimed the camera,

and posed himself, eyes closed and body leaning slightly
against a chair to make it heavy, to give it the stillness

of a corpse, it's probable he fell asleep, so unblurred is
his torso with clasped hands, his combed wet hair.

Bayard claims on the back of the 1840 photograph
that the body is drowned, tells how

the French government overlooked him for Daguerre
and how no one claimed the body from the morgue,

photography's first self-portrait a faked suicide with a note ending:
"Ladies and gentlemen, pass on lest he offend your sense of smell."

When I first saw death I felt my body freeze, I felt how hard
to keep the mind still, how hard to understand, relive,

undo the moment when the falling body
made no sound, a split second in the corner of my eye,

then nothing in the chalky sky but the tip of an apartment building.
Then a gasping, then the body hidden by a circle of bystanders

taking uneven steps back as the blood began to pool,
as the blood itself grew fingers

releasing something that cold February morning.
So hard to hold the body still, at the stairway to the metro

my breath billowed out. A policeman grabbed my shoulders
and yelled for me to stop, he held me there

to keep me and the rest of the crowd away from the body,
yelled *"Arrêtez!"* while the blood on the pavement

became a kind of cursive, a story told
on the sidewalk's pages of dying and exposure.

Waiting to Wake Up *Française*

After kirs in tall glasses at the Café Dupon,
we roamed the cobblestone streets, each
storefront window a stage, empty save for its props
and the dark behind them. A *boulangerie*
every block, five blocks to the bus stop.
He'd persuade me to go in his Peugeot,
a silver compact stick shift. Angers at night was
a spotless ghetto of thin white buildings,
no midnight, no field there, billboards
unfamiliar with the frenzy of circumflexes
and *accents graves*. The car left running
at my door, Vincent's hand suddenly at the small
of my back, my knee knocking the gear shift,
his throat choking something trite but
passionate, "*Tu me craques*," a matchstick
flaring, far-off tires squealing, our faces gone blue
under the streetlamp. No familiarity
even in the way lip pressed lip,
I decided to be untouchable, never
to drag my fingers down the back of a man's
shaved neck. Nor to speak of what blackened
like numbers on the oval license plate's
fine glitter. The town, whose markets sold
flowers and paperbacks of Proust,
turned frightening. American films
became oddities I refused to see, denied them
like Peter. Outside nameless cafés
crowded with canvas umbrellas, I sat holding
a café noir too bitter to drink.
Sugar cube balanced at the rim of the cup,
I watched the dark bleed through
until it crumbled. I read Irish poetry,

curled pages of a journal pressing too hard
as I wrote, words half French, half American.
In bed, I contemplated defenestration,
laughter, abuse. I turned each away.

Dear John Bunyan,

To you I admit I never read
Pilgrim's Progress, although once
I bought the Cliffs Notes in a Paris bookstore
and circled the boulevard, feverish
in a winter coat, waiting for Benoît while
your pilgrim, I read, was cudgeled
by a crabtree. In the café,
I didn't kiss Benoît to whom I'd made love
in the fountain at Saint Sulpice,
though we held hands
as I told him your allegorical plot
and to him I confessed what
I realized later he knew—
I was no pilgrim.

I've dreamt of you for two winters,
your runny nose, a grin
widening to your ears, chafed and kindled.
I'm the invisible observer of your
twilight seizures in the belfry,
body smashed to the floor as you
listen ecstatically to God's heavy black call.
Still, you persist, fearful as the bell swings
it will fall on you, for your death you knew
from nightmare to be a breathless iron cage.
Your friends are brain-sick fellows,
your angels, the paranoid.
So you hide in the rafters, long
after dark, you pray and spot angels
in the sky like deaf familiar stars,
and the angels, frenzied by your despondency,
make all the churches flood, water
rising until we are "likely to have drowned

nine or ten times," and always there
I desert you, waking.

What could recall the bell's swing but your
own knee jerking? Were you a sinner, John,
or were you merely cold? In the Jardin Luxembourg
rainstorms pulled petals off shrubs like tufts of soft hair.
I kiss cold air as if it were heated
by the loved one's lungs—despite the shiver—
homesick at the gate's edge of the garden,
mad with God-fearing.

Jazz in Paris

is a wet blue street, an American name
cartoonish in a Parisian arrondissement,
    a dance floor packed with chairs
where I slip into some form of listening
    that requires almost no movement and
looking around I see women
    leaning toward, in the arms of
men smoking cigarettes in tight leather jackets.

The musicians speak to the crowd
in English, making my accent lazy
    when the waiter comes around.
If I don't pour the beer in a glass I may be thrown out
    for behaving "*provocateur.*" I want to be
back in New Orleans, stamping cigarettes out
    on the dark wood floor of Tipitina's
under fans that don't do the job once the people arrive,
    I want to be down by Armstrong Park,
where the best stuff is: Joe's Cozy Corner, Russell's Cool Spot,
    the Little People's Place with free red beans and
seats on barrels in a dark room riddled with bent knees
    and trumpets aimed at ceilings
(not the "*oui, oui*" of the waiter).

My body slouches and two fingers dreamily
cradle a cigarette, knowing what it means to miss . . .
    all that brass gleaming under red lights,
making you feel rich. Serious French cool cats
    slurp appreciations: "*C'est hip, non?*
C'est happening!" Fingers snapping.
    When I first heard Nina Simone's
"Ne Me Quitte Pas," I heard it sung by a man at his most pathetic:
    Laisse-moi devenir l'ombre de ton ombre . . .

I subscribed to this pleading long ago and so
    —let me become the shadow of your shadow—
the drunk Frenchman lying across the table
      hamming up "Ne Me Quitte Pas" didn't startle me.
The olive garnishes he sent rolling off the tablecloth
      and across the floor didn't startle me.
What did: my private desires broadcast through horns,
      gleaming in gin glasses across the room.

Boulevard Slick with Rain

In the blue light, each of us looks
    For a place we belong.
We don't know how far
    We'll have to walk to catch the metro.

Our shoes scrape against the sidewalk,
    Jan's hand squeezing mine. We fight
Over who carries the suitcase, my black dress
    Stuffed inside for her father's funeral.

Jan wants the weight in her hand.
    Like the painter who carried his portrait under his arm,
As if he might revise it anywhere. Not his fresco
    Fixed in a monastery, where a woman

In a surgical mask studies the palimpsest of dust
    And candle smoke, tries to undo
The damage of hundreds of years.
    It is twilight, all boundary, and the boulevard

Is ribbon winding slowly lighter—*entre chien et loup.*
    Pigeons strut at the iron gate, restless,
And the boulevard is slick with rain.
    Jan searches her coin purse for francs.

The street funnels the headlights
    From cars, holds them, arranges them in long lines,
Red and white and yellow, our shoes
    Extinguishing the light beneath the sfumato air.

The sidewalk glows metallic—I could go on:
    It silvers, reflects sky. And the artist
With his rolled-up canvas, his brush and egg yolk,
    Perhaps he wanted to preserve this light

Our shoes press into or
        The way we watch a man
Walk to his car, unlock the door,
        Light in his hair as he climbs in,

Gesture of stretching seatbelt, door slam.
        How can we preserve any of this?
Coughing of engine, white reverse lights,
        His head twists backward as

My lips try to brighten Jan's face with a kiss.
        A woman restores the fresco, one square
Inch per month, and we see the entrance to the metro
        As the boulevard unravels beneath our feet.

Arrival in Rome

1
My head aches, and the stale air burns
    My throat, pricks me into sweat and dream.
The train rushes its heavy skeleton, shakes
    My head side to side in half-paralysis
— The nimbus state of half-sleep — and when
    I open my eyes, feverish, near laughter,
        The blur of lights far off — Venice — carnival
            With men in top hats,
        Women dressed as harlequins or
            Divas or fat fuzzy bees.

2
How impossible it is to be alone,
    Not to be seen, impossible not
To look, even in fever to give oneself up
    To not looking, to close the eyes for sleep
In this paradox of stillness and movement,
    To be prone and yet hurtling through the dark
        That presses against the compartment's windows
            While a couple whispers in the aisle.
        To know there is always something beyond
            And to fear that one may never arrive.

3
You appeared like a gargoyle floating in the corner
    Of my room, beseeched "Sink not Lethe-ward!"
By day my tongue stuttered French, grew
    Proficient, never graceful. In France I was
Never beautiful. I rose on cold mornings,
    Ate oatmeal cooked in my one pot, served in
        My one bowl, eaten with my filched spoon.
        I would reflect the world.
        I promised myself I would find you,
            I would glow my uncertainty like the moon.

4

I let them fetch the dusty books of letters
    From the hidden stacks of the Sorbonne.
Under windows letting in the city's dark
    I was one woman amid the hundred
Tables and lamps. All winter I read.
        You prayed like a heathen to your Venus star,
            The nightingale could sing even as it flew.
                I prayed to you.
            I can't explain why I thought you loved me too.
                "That which is creative must create itself."

5

Darling, you have been my sweetest companion,
    And for many a time I have been in love
With this in-between, volleyed back and forth,
    Never able to know the *now* escaping
Like water moving through fingers. Now
        More than ever it seems impossible
            To unthink the lover's hot breath against
                The cheek, the ear, to brush
            One's face up against the *now*, close
                One's eyes and be carried off to bed.

6

Oh, to arrive in Rome! where you go
    To die and I to find you, to walk the streets
With tourists and taxis, the lemony light off
    Ivory buildings, to stare at Moses with his horns,
At Apollo chasing Daphne as she twists
        Into branches. All that moves will later
            Freeze: the death mask of your face.
                I'll remember your letters,
            Every word I can conjure:
                "The tears will come to your eyes. Let them."

7

Fog, first a little, then wind blowing it
 Up and away those mornings I trudged
Through the gardens, past the big-bellied Balzac
 On Boulevard Raspail. You were nowhere.
My breath billowed out in clouds of steam,
 Unable to be controlled, almost embarrassing.
  The train cries out. It is nearly dawn.
   The fever breaks and takes
  You with it. You were with me, palpable.
   In the rattling, I am waiting to arrive.

IV

The Train

When at night I hear the train go by
in strokes and sobs, I know we will remain

still and hardened in our beds. The cry
of the train spreads through the low field and houses

that could all silently be on fire.
I do not want to fall asleep again

and miss the moment that cannot last and yet
(my love my love my love my almost lamplight)

when the train divides the night
I sink like a suitcase filled with nails.

Summary

There was a bar in a smelly basement,
beer foam lining two plastic cups. There was
a bite on the neck, on the soft inside

of the arm, a crude joke and two or three
flattened pillows. Then your heart-carved
face, a wild laugh he lit with matchsticks.

There were politics, and they surfaced
like black outlines. There was one kiss,
caught in a photograph and taped to the mirror.

There was a foreign country, a new currency,
there was a nightmare of running,
the bright explosion of his face, there were

his eyelids, stretched closed, his hand
clasping cover, and by the bed, piles of T-shirts
in hot weather, wool socks in winter.

Spices filled a yellow kitchen. There was never
a promise to stay, words said and words you wanted
to mean. A departure, a refrigerator door ajar,

a return. Refusals and cigarette ash in the sink.
There were many nervous habits, therapists
and movie plots, paint and dancing. Promises,

but not to stay. A shaky nod of the head,
straw wrappers and bottle caps. A pause.
A postal holiday. Lies and gossip.

Steam in the pots, water and wine
in a glass. Teeth and stomach.
A present tense didn't apply to the moment.

Cusp

Cusp of sleep   the body supine
Between what is   right and also
Errant in an open field   unpredictable wind and sunlight
Before sleep one abandons   the lover
The body of a man   turns foreign
Echoes   the risk of falling
(Who will pay   attention to the mouth
Warm   without memory)
Stopped   or traveling
It was all one could do   not to

Self-Portrait as *Annunciation*

1
Behind him there is the stuttering applause
    of a waterfall against clay-smelling steps. It is early spring
and sunlight anchors the silver branches
    to stone shadows. The light shifts infinitesimally
at the threshold of the toy-like architecture, where the Madonna
    tires of her book,

2
squeezes her eyes thin. The messenger eyes her softly, fully,
    unwinds the scroll upward, unspools toward her
like a magic carpet.

3
The words in gothic script, printed upside down for God in heaven
to read.

4
Because he has come to the threshold, to the tiny staircase,

5
Isaiah's prophecies, *Mary, do not be afraid,* lay in the darkness of
    her closed book while the messenger's scroll
flies toward

6
her face. Gnats float like dust motes
    in the air between (I volleyed back and forth)
the looping new branches, and to what end?

7
Why can we not say she will make of her whole body . . . attentive.
    She raises her almond-shaped hands, she pulls the fear
out of her breast like a wrinkled ribbon

8
but the scroll is interminable, unmanageable, fire lit in
    sunlight, its base invisible, its gas tip . . .

9
She squints won't-you-please-leave-me-alone,
    raises her hand to cover her face.
(Didn't I once love my own fear?)

10
The messenger has come to the threshold:
    he lowers his chin to target her
in his uninterruptible gaze, his piecing the beginning
    to the ending, his delivering, his handing over,
can he mouth this over?

11
And will she be object, then garment, then art, be emptied?

12
Will she hold it? How will she dismantle the nest
    in her ribcage while birds shriek above
the waterfall? The messenger's mouth agape, her eyes
    angled skyward.

13
If he ceases to issue the message,
    who will be her mirror?
(All of the ways I help you leave.)
    She will make of her whole body an ear.

The Wolf

It was dawn when the wolf turned away from me,
his paw in a steel trap. Though I admire wakers
swimming up to the surface toward sky—the clear,
dry ocean of the mind—I sank back.

His paw bloodied in unretractable teeth,
I was able only to loosen the trap from its chain.
He circled the tree with clatter and limping.
When he fell, exhausted, the trap's jaw opened.

The pack of wolves approached swiftly then,
their silence devastating amid the scuffing leaves.
I knew what would happen, I heard each heavy pant
as the wolves lined up. The sleep was torn, reentered . . .

When he comes back like an animal, when he runs like one
able to hear far-off cries, then he is most lost to me.

The Train, 2

I listen for trains, for the dark arms that bless
the fields. For grooved wheels, pipes and steam,
an organ echo. Asking night's thick dream
to answer, the train speaks transit, the billowy mess
of moaning smoke. *Where were we, yes,*
before we were here? The train is not my whim
for flight. It speaks. The headlight's gleam
prepares the freight behind it, will confess
all its numbers and railings to blurry ground
lost beneath its links. We couldn't hold
it all, remember all of it, bound like coal
fevering the engine room. I tell you
we were always here, how we found
ourselves still at dawn, hardly consoled.

Mind of Winter

Along the downtown streets, shards
of glass and ice are indistinguishable,
and trees lining the square
strain to lift their branches.

This is what we asked for: a miserable walk
to view the runny mélange of city
now fused and crystalline.
The gloved hand feels for solace

while all outdoors is glazed
in the half-inch of ice light,
black and silver streamers
that garland every lonely thing,

touch the telephone pole, wrapped in concert
fliers, skate the sidewalk, steps, curb and
handrail, brush the car doors, doorknobs.
Do you see, we don't belong.

Like the blackbirds slipping
off the wire fence, we peck and tiptoe
in the crackling grass. Solace
could be mistaken for another grief,

but it's to be found before the melt,
before each pearl spotting the branches
drips down to release the *now*. Time
stopped, I say, and we do not belong.

Inevitable

Not the knife's gleam jutting from a hand under a streetlamp,
Not the sound of rock shattering the second-story window
But the panic one feels in a car stopped on the highway.
 The repeating

Blip of brake lights, the foot growing tired on the clutch and brake.
Ahead, a truck carrying a load of windshields has crashed.
A patience wears thin, a dancer with a ripped-up skirt.

To talk about fear this way is nearly futile: a patience wears thin,
And real fear emerges, not the snapping of glass under tires,
 the ambulance lights
Careening into twilight, but the glass and light that bring

A trembling loyal to my fingers. My fear is a vigil
In which I contemplate whether what will happen is inevitable.
I succeed in being lost, waiting behind the windshield flooded
 with glare.

Elegy

Because it's still there, syrupy light
on the roads, indigo foils
the sunset in the aftermath
of rainstorm. Transience,

did you get away? I have watched
the sunset long enough to learn its nuance,
its surreptitious shoveling of dark,
poured deepest into bare branches

of trees and long arms of cranes
and electric poles. But it is ruinous
here by the swelling river:
the still life of docks and

stevedoring is rusting metal
too complicated to decipher
and even now you are the steep bridge
of cast-iron fretwork crossing the Ohio,

a strobing prison I drive beneath.
If this is the last poem I will write for you,
how can I finish? I love these
frayed strips of tire rubber on their backs

like dying insects, the slight
distinctions of speed cars trade
under the kaleidoscopic prism
of road signs. If art loses

its creative drive the moment it is
separated from worship, then
what can I tell you? What
annunciation do we allow for the end?

What's left to confess makes me
hold my breath: you are
the thick white smoke issuing
from the factory, my Louisville skyline,

backdropped by the Ohio's black ripples,
the Colgate sign, red neon
with synchronized tubes
flashing off and on to form

a tableau vivant in which
the viewer believes in movement
while it is all stasis
and paradox to worship.

Between Dog and Wolf

I can't help but look back: piles of rusted stakes
half buried in the ground which gives after the melt.

The train cars are disconnected, paralyzed
on their tracks, empty but for cold. The train

is dangerous and sleepy. I listen for its two
appearances which fill my upstairs room:

the tired horns of 5 P.M., hazy with downtown traffic
and the heartbreaking roar of its 1 A.M. passage.

Between the dog and the wolf
signifies twilight. That moment when

the dog has wandered all day and is tired
and the wolf has just woken to roam.

My perspective for holding the world
grows remote, compelling but archaic

like these cabooses parked near the trees.
Once their engines were needed for old trains

heavy with cargo. Now front engines pull
the cars, make the friction of wheels spinning sparks.

What does it mean that trains no longer
need to be pushed and pulled to glide?

Patches of snow go pink in the finishing sun
and the dog and the wolf, both ravenous,

are on either side of the tracks. When the train derails,
it chooses which side. My life has already seen

the technology abandoned by the century, but transience
comes from the animal world, like the mayflies

whose lives are an eyeblink, whose birth, metamorphosis,
mating in air and plummeting into water take place

between dog and wolf. I have found enough clues
to bury my heart. But I have loved you into the fourth season.

I am therefore moved by the abandoned train cars,
the gunmetal gray of the macadam, the train as it charges

toward—not an end so much as an acceptance.
My gifts, my undeserved, precious receipts.

Bread Loaf and the Bakeless Prizes

SINCE 1926 the Bread Loaf Writers' Conference has convened every August in the shadow of Bread Loaf Mountain, in Vermont's Green Mountains, where Middlebury College maintains a summer campus. The conference, founded by Robert Frost and Willa Cather—a generation before creative writing became a popular course of study—brings together established poets and prose writers, editors, and literary agents to work with writers at various stages of their careers.

While part of Bread Loaf's reputation was built on the writers associated with it—W. H. Auden, Wallace Stegner, Katherine Anne Porter, Toni Morrison, and Adrienne Rich, to name a few—it has an equally high reputation for finding and supporting writers of promise in the earliest stages of their careers. Eudora Welty, Carson McCullers, Anne Sexton, May Swenson, Russell Banks, Joan Didion, Richard Ford, Julia Alvarez, Carolyn Forché, Linda Pastan, Ellen Bryant Voigt, Andrea Barrett, and Tim O'Brien are some of the poets, novelists, and short story writers who benefited from early associations with Bread Loaf.

There are many obstacles to a successful literary career, but none is more difficult to overcome than the publication of a first book. The Katharine Bakeless Nason Literary Publication Prizes were established in 1995 to expand Bread Loaf's commitment to the support of emerging writers. Endowed by the LZ Francis Foundation, whose directors wished to commemorate Middlebury College patron Katharine Bakeless Nason and to encourage emerging writers, the Bakeless Prizes launch the publication career of a poet, fiction writer, and creative nonfiction writer annually. Winning manuscripts are chosen in an open national competition by a distinguished judge in each genre. (Past judges include Andrea Barrett, Ursula Hegi, Francine Prose, Edward Hirsch, Tomas Mallon, Louise Glück, and Yusef Komunyakaa.) The winning books are published in August to coincide with the Bread Loaf Writers' Conference, and the authors are invited to participate as Bakeless Fellows.

Since they first appeared in 1996, the winning Bakeless books have been critical successes. As a result, the Bakeless Prizes are coveted among new writers. The fact that Houghton Mifflin publishes these books is significant, for it joins together one of America's oldest and most distinguished literary presses with an equally distinguished writers' conference. The collaboration speaks to the commitment of both institutions to cultivate emerging literary artists in order to ensure a richer future for American writing.

MICHAEL COLLIER
Director, Bread Loaf Writers' Conference